The Birthing Position of an Intercessor

Frances Cleveland

The Birthing Position of an Intercessor

Copyright© 2005 Frances Cleveland

Hannah's Sons and Daughters
C/O Breaking of Day Family Church
P. O. Box 2811
DeSoto, TX 75123-2811
bodfc@yahoo.com
htpp://www.hannahssonsanddaughters.com

Catalogued in the Library of Congress—Publication Data

ISBN 978-0615628370

Printed in the United States of America

Printing and Editorial Services
Clark's Graphics and Publications
Clarkspublications@comcast.net
972-424-2074 (Office)
972-424-2074 (Fax)

Dedication

This book is dedicated to my precious mother, Rita Faye Johnson, who instilled so much wisdom in me. You were always "drilling" in me to be the best, and that I could be whatever I purpose within my heart to be. I love you, "Mama."

To my husband, Apostle Donald E. Cleveland, Sr., who is the wind beneath my wings. You have released me to triumph wondrously in all that the Lord has predestined for my life. I love you with all my heart. I also dedicate this book to my beautiful three sons and grandchildren, and their generation to come. Also, my beautiful daughter-in-law, Janice Cleveland. I pray that the words that are expressed in the pages of this book will provoke all of you to seek the Lord with a greater intensity and to position yourselves in His face for His glory. I thank God for lending you all to me.

I dedicate this book to my best friend, Wanda Hugger, who has gone to be with the Lord. Today, I believe, she is one of the saints in the great clouds of witnesses who is cheering me on and saying, "Frances, go ahead." She was a mighty intercessor and my mentor. I miss you, Wanda.

I also dedicate this book to my friend, Prophet Richard Evans, who the Lord used when I was in the valley of decision to lay his hand on me to bring forth the destiny that was ordained for me from the foundation of the world. I am now at a pivotal point in my life and the Lord is now fulfilling that in which you spoke of concerning the great patriarch, Hannah, into my life. I bless you with all the power that the Lord has invested within me as His prophetess.

Finally, to my spiritual mother in the Lord, Mother Queen Esther Jones, who the Lord saw fit to call home. There is a lasting imprint in my life that can never be erased of how you were constantly saying, "Sister Cleveland, the half has not been told." I thank God for Him letting you share the last days of your life pouring into me. Mother, I miss you.

CONTENTS

Special Acknowledgements

With great appreciation and love I acknowledge my Lord and Savior Jesus Christ; God, who is my Almighty Father and friend, and the Holy Spirit for being my guidance and giving me a wealth of wisdom.

I would also like to express my appreciation to the following:

To Breaking of Day Family Church, who supports me in every endeavor that the Lord has entrusted into my hand.

Pastor Donald and Lady Gina Smith of Harvest Church in Fort Worth, Texas, who has unselfishly given unto my ministry and have not looked for anything in return. Thank you, Pastor Smith, for so graciously sowing into my life by permitting Lady Gina to deposit her expertise and resources into my life.

I especially thank Regina Hill for seeing the vision and saying to me as Deborah said to Barak, "What has the Lord told you to do?" You have been the instrument that I have prayed for to catapult my ministry to a new dimension.

Last, but not least, Dr. Shirley Clark of Jabez Prayer Network in Plano, Texas for being a friend who saw the pen of a ready writer in me and without restraints made available all of her resources so that the author in me could be released and brought forth to the Kingdom of God.

.

Foreword

What a wonderful time in which we are living, a time and a generation where God is revealing and unveiling information and revelation of His mandate and agenda concerning the divine purpose and divine providence of His will.

From the beginning of civilization, it was the desire of God that mankind would glorify Him through obedience. Because man allowed evil to invade his heart, which produced sin, judgment came, but God had a plan to rescue and redeem man from the destruction of sin. Thanks be to God and all praises goes to Him. For over two thousand years ago the redeemer, Jesus Christ, came and paid the ultimate price with the shedding of His blood.

Yet God's people and creation are plagued with evil, demonic forces and powers that have been determined to steal, kill and destroy what God has purposed and ordained for His people.

There are strategies, principles and dynamics that have been revealed to reverse the curse so that we might survive the onslaughts of the enemy. Prophetess Frances Cleveland has stated emphatically in her book, *"The Birthing Position of A Intercessor"* (*Travailing To Birth Divine Purpose in the New Millennium),* that intercessory prayer is one of the key ingredients to survival. Every child of God must read this book.

For over twenty years God has taught and used Prophetess Frances Cleveland to usher His people into a level and dimension of intercessory prayer, perhaps they have never experienced.

Not only are the Daughters of God (Hannah's Daughters), but the Sons (Hannah's Sons) are hearing the clarion call to prayer, and to weep and travail between the porch and the altar. There is a birthing in the spirit taking place and this is the last hour.

Prophetess Cleveland is being used as a midwife to help deliver the baby of purpose and destiny. I consider this book a prenatal and after care manual that teaches us how to nurture, develop and protect that which the Holy Ghost has impregnated within us.

I thank God for my wife allowing God to birth this invaluable treasure and make it accessible to those that understand the power of this unveiled, revealed, revelation and information that empowers and causes God's people to abound triumphantly.

Apostle Donald E. Cleveland, Sr.
Breaking Of Day Family Church, Senior Pastor

Chapter One
The Travail of the Spirit

Webster's Collegiate Dictionary defines travail as work of a painful or laborious nature; toil; a physical or mental exertion or piece of work. A task, effort, agony, torment, labor or parturition. In so many words, travail is a type of laborious, toiling and agonizing within one's spirit. So when we look at travail in regards to intercession and intercessors, this is exactly what one will experience when birthing God's purpose in the earth through prayer.

In John 11:33-44, you will see one of the episodes in Jesus' life when He was in travail. Verse 33 says Jesus groaned in the spirit, and was troubled. A more literal translation of this verse is that Jesus "was moved with indignation in His spirit and deeply troubled." And another translation says it this say, "Jesus was deeply moved in spirit." The word "troubled" is tarasso in the Greek. It means "to stir or agitate" like a washing machine has an agitator. Through Jesus' indignation the anointing was being stirred up in Him.

Jesus' tears were not only tears of sympathy, but indignation and the stirring of His spirit. We also know this happened during the time He was in prayer. Verse 41 points out that He was praying to His Father, "I thank thee that thou hast heard me." Then He said, "Lazarus come forth."

I believe at this time by the revelation of the spirit that He was travailing. Because Webster defines travail as work or exertion and that it is laborious in nature. Groaning is a sign that Jesus' spirit was in a laborious mode. Travail is not always determined by the weeping and groaning of spirit, but the spirit will show up with some type of fervency when one is in deep intercession. As we see in Jesus' example.

I remember when the Lord woke me up through the probing of the spirit and called me to a time of deep intercession. I was groaning and weeping. It seemed that my very insides were hurting. I was balled up in a fetal position and rebuking the spirit of death. I saw a vision of two men fighting, one was overtaking the other. I commanded the spirit of death to be rebuked. I interceded for about an hour. After this period of prevailing in prayer, the Lord spoke to me and said that it was done.

About three months later, my father died. Before his death, he was in route to make it home to see me. Unfortunately, he did not make it. At that time, I thought he had not given his life to the Lord. I was very distraught and tormented in my mind. I told the Lord, "You said that You would deliver my father." He spoke to me so profoundly and said, "Yes, I promised that I would deliver him, and I did."

Before we had the funeral my aunt called me and told me that my father was trying to make it home to me when he became deathly ill. During the time of his encounter with death, he gave his life to the Lord. You see the vision that I had of the two men fighting, one of them was my father and the other death. Because of my obedience to position myself before the Lord through the birthing of the spirit with travailing prayer, my father was received into God's kingdom. Hallelujah, praise God.

When we travail in prayer, it does not always happen quickly, but you have to consistently knock on Heaven's door, knowing that the Lord's purpose will be birthed in your situation.

Jesus was in travail of spirit in the Garden of Gethsemane for the redemption of mankind. However, His work of intercession for mankind began with His travail in the garden. It was prophesied by Isaiah, in Isaiah 53:11, that "He shall see of the travail of his soul and shall be satisfied."

In Matthew 26:38 Jesus said, "My soul is exceeding sorrowful, even unto death." The redemptive power of the Holy Spirit prevailed through the power of Christ's intercession in the Garden of Gethsemane and the victory was won.

During the process of Christ's travail, redemption was taking place. The scriptures declare that Jesus was sweating so profusely that it was like a person bleeding. There's a medical condition called hematidrosis. The blood that was shed through the pores of His skin was the beginning process of bringing lost humanity back to God.

The Rain of the Spirit

Before the Lord's purpose is brought forth in a situation on the earth, He always used a vessel to intercede in prayer before His plan was implemented. Elijah was a man of passion such as we are. He prophesied to King Ahab that by a space of three and a half years that it wouldn't rain on the earth. This was a judgment sent by God because of Israel's disobedience and the sin of idolatry. The land was depleted of its resources and many died of starvation.

Through divine intervention and God's mercy for mankind, the Lord sent rain after three and a half years. We know that it was God's timing, but still He needed a vessel to intercede and birth the rain of the spirit.

In I Kings 18, we see Elijah praying seven times for rain. When he was praying his posture was in a position as a woman giving birth. This shows that his spirit was in travail. He was birthing rain. I believe this is the reason why God gives us the illustration of the position he was in while praying.

Just as Israel had a natural drought and through the travailing and birthing prayer of Elijah, the Lord sent His divine purpose for rain on the earth. He will also use our travail of the spirit in prayer to send His latter rain on a spiritually dry church. Our prayers release the Holy Spirit to move in situations where He will produce life. This is called the Hovering of the Holy Spirit. When we pray for souls to be birthed into the kingdom of God, we release the rain or birthing of the spirit to go and hover over that soul and it releases life.

Just as Elijah dared to position himself before the Lord, we can also pull on the altar of prayer and release God's hand in our situation. When I'm in prayer on Monday nights with a prayer group; which the Lord has charged me to call them Hannah's Sons and Daughters, I tell them to push until something happens.

When we push to the point where the people of God are travailing with such intensity in the spirit, we are able to see people's lives loosed from bondages and shackles broken off of them. I liken this experience to a woman giving birth to a baby, and before the baby is born, the water breaks. This is what the scriptures say in Roman 8:26, "Likewise the Spirit also helpeth our infirmities: for we know not what we should pray for as we ought: but the Spirit itself maketh intercession for us with groaning which cannot be uttered."

The Lord is about to send the latter rain of His glory upon His people, and He is going to always have a remnant that is going to do great exploits in Him. The people who know their God shall be strong and do great exploits. Intercessors, keep pursuing God until He sends the rain of His glory amongst His people—that many souls will be loosed through the travail of the spirit, so that God's divine purpose will be done in their lives.

Chapter Two
21 Days of Holy Consecration

In the book of Daniel the 10th chapter, we see Daniel humbling himself before the Lord, seeking Him with 21 days of fasting and prayer. While he was on the consecration before the Lord, his prayers were answered. The angel of the Lord appeared to him and said, "Fear not Daniel for from the first day that thou didst set thine heart to understand, and to chasten thyself before thy God, thy words were heard, and I am come for thy words. But the prince of the kingdom of Persia withstood me one and twenty days." Daniel humbled his soul to the point that Jesus, the Son of Man, appeared unto him. He received a mighty breakthrough and prophetic revelation of his vision.

When we seek the Lord as intercessors, there will come a season in our lives when the devil will come to withstand the answer to our prayers. We had an experience like this in our prayer ministry. We had been seeking God for four and a half years, with gut-wrenching travailing prayers, but it seemed as though all Heaven was shut up.

After making the assessment and discerning in the spirit that the intercessors (Hannah's Sons and Daughters) were experiencing this kind of hindrance from the devil, the Lord revealed to me that there would be a mighty breakthrough now for His people.

In the month of January 2005, I called for a solemn assembly with 21 days of fasting and prayer. While we were seeking the face of the Lord, I had a vision. In the vision, I was flying over telephone lines, trees and tall buildings. I was soaring like an eagle. There were dogs pursuing the people of God. I had a whip in my hand to fight them off. There were all kinds of obstacles to conquer, and every time I was confronted with one, I triumphed. The Lord spoke to me during the consecration to tell the people that we were going to experience trials and tribulations, but we would soar like an eagle and prevail. Because I had the whip of deliverance in my hand, I would be the one that the Lord would use to help bring deliverance.

During the time of humbling ourselves before the Lord, He sent a mighty outpouring of His spirit to refresh and renew our commitment unto Him. Many of the Saints received mighty deliverance through their health, finances, marriage and many other areas in their lives. Also, we encountered many obstacles and trials. Just as the Lord spoke concerning the attack of the enemy, it was so as well. But what victories we have experienced through it all. Just as Daniel prevailed, we also prevailed. People who had been driving inferior cars, experiencing failing health, and living in houses that were only temporary, started receiving breakthroughs that only God could give.

Fasting and praying with intensity will bring you into the face of adversity, but your sacrifice will render the enemy defeated every time. Fasting will bring supernatural powers of deliverance. It will take you into the throne room of God and touch the hem of His garment and it will bring His mighty virtue and power that will cause the captive to be set free. We should not fast as the heathen do to let our voice be heard on high, but when we fast we shouldn't appear unto men to fast, but in secret unto the Father; and our Father, which seeth in secret, shall reward thee openly.

In Matthew 6:18, it shows that fasting will afflict the soul. This type of sacrifice says to God, nothing else matters at this point, but a word and a visitation from Him. If you receive a word from Him, you will know what to do. Isaiah 58:6 says, "Is not this the fast that I have chosen? to loose the bands of wickedness to undo the heavy burdens, and to let the oppressed go free, and that ye break every yoke?" The eighth verse says, "Then shall thy light break forth as the morning and thine health shall spring forth speedily: and thy righteousness shall go before thee: the glory of the Lord shall be thy rearward."

When you set your heart to fast or the Lord calls you to one, you must determine which fast you will commit unto the Lord. Fasting is going without that which is pleasant to the senses. It is not just going without food. It is going without that which is pleasant and satisfying to the flesh. Just going without food and not setting a time and place to commune with God for a period of time is not a fast that He has chosen. Concentrate on Him at the time you have committed unto Him and your spirit will be illuminated and you will experience His supernatural presence in your life.

He wants our uncomplicated allegiance. He wants to have His way with His hungry followers. He reminds us to pause often in His presence, remove the physical food from before us and replace it with the bread that satisfies eternally, promoting healing of the spirit; which promises that we will never experience dryness as long as we thirst for Him. A time of intimacy with God will always bring an outward manifestation of His glory and it will project to everyone who comes near you that you have been with Him.

Consecration of the Priesthood

1 Peter 2:9 says, "But ye are a chosen generation, a royal priesthood, and holy nation, a peculiar people, that ye should show forth the

praises of him who hath called you out of darkness into his marvelous light."

When the Lord saves a person, He consecrates them unto His royal priesthood. We no longer have to go to the priest to enter the Holy Place. Because of the victory that was won on the cross at Calvary, we can go boldly to the throne of grace that we may obtain mercy and find grace to help in the time of need. The word, "consecration" means to set apart. This should be a ongoing act toward God. We should present a life that is separated for His use.

This was done in the case when God told Moses to set aside Aaron and his sons, Nadab, Abihu, Eleazar and Ithamar. Exodus 28:41 records it this way, "And thou shalt put them, (priestly garments) upon Aaron thy brother, and his sons with him; and shalt anoint them, and consecrate them, and sanctify them, that they may minister unto me in the priest's office." This was the initial consecration.

Then there are other times when God calls us to set aside some sacrificial time before Him. I find in my life that whenever He requires this kind of consecration from me, He's about to break yokes and bring deliverance in my life or the situation that I'm interceding for during this time.

Praise God for the consecrated life that we can have before Him. We should always have a life of consecration before Him, so that when He lets down the golden scepter to beckon us to come near unto Him to share a time of intimacy beyond the veil, we will cry, "Here I am Lord, your servant will obey."

Chapter Three

Seek To Enter Into His Presence

*I*t is the deep roots produced in *private* fellowship that brings power for public benefit. Jesus was led by the Holy Spirit into the wilderness (Luke 4). When He returned, He came in the power of the Spirit. He was led into a time of fasting and prayer before beginning His public ministry.

If only each young believer could learn from the beginning of his or her Christian walk, the importance of this truth. *If Jesus Himself needed to go into the presence of His Father to be renewed and find guidance, how much more does today's child of God need to do this?*

As you enter into God's presence in worship and shut out the distractions of your mind, you step into the Holy of Holies. It is the sanctuary of the Lord, and you enter in spirit to the place of nearness to God. In Ezekiel 44:15, 16, we find priests who were faithful to minister unto God in the sanctuary.

But the priests, the Levites, the sons of Zadok, that kept the charge of my sanctuary when the children of Israel went astray from me, they shall come near to me to minister unto me, and they shall stand before me to offer unto me the fat and the blood, saith the Lord God:

They shall enter into my sanctuary, and they shall come near to my table, to minister unto me, and they shall keep my charge.

Those who maintain the attitude that ministering unto the Lord first is essential will be those who enter into deep and intimate service to the Lord.

These sons of Zadok continued to enter the sanctuary even when others had abandoned God. They were told not to wear anything into the inner court that caused them to perspire. So when they went into the outer court to minister to the people, the clothes they wore while ministering to Him in the bedchambers were left behind, so they would not become contaminated.

When you come into His presence, know that Jesus has already gone before you to prepare the way. You can enter with complete confidence that you belong because He has given you His robe of righteousness through your simple faith in Him. It is not by your own perspiration, not even your work for God that brings you near to Him, but only by your confidence in Jesus's sacrifice and a willingness to enter.

He said, "They shall come near to me to minister to me." This is service to God that can be done no other way. You must come before Him. You cannot serve Him from a distance. The outer court is where you approach people, but the inner court is where you approach God.

Many times we feel that all we do in the outer court gives us a good excuse for not drawing near to God in the inner court. But without closeness to God through fellowship and through ministry to Him in your bedchamber, you will find that your busyness with people— even ministry to them—is being done more to gratify your flesh than to build the Kingdom of God.

It seems for the most part that there is a lot of sweat in today's ministries and little waiting quietly in the presence of God to obtain His counsel and wisdom.

Your inner man will determine your output. If you will simply allow God to open your life and draw you close to Him, His very presence will saturate you with His influence. He will put in you the things that He wants to flow through you. It becomes a beautiful relationship that continues to increase as you become comfortable being alone with Him.

The Bed Chamber

No words can express the zenith and splendor that is waiting for us in God's bedchamber. Only those who continue to press toward God's heart with intimacy will find their place in Him. Everyone who longs for and lingers at the feet of Jesus with deep communion will experience a relationship with Him. God longs for us to pursue Him passionately, not just having casual visits with Him. In His bedchamber (The Holy Place) is where He tells us His deepest thoughts; thus, trust us to hold onto Him in prayer until our prayers move Him to answer. Just like in the natural. You only let those who are intimate and close to you know secret things about you. It is the same with God. He says in Deuteronomy 29:29, "The secret things belong unto the Lord our God: but those things, which are revealed, belong unto us and our children forever, that we may do all the words of this law."

In the book of Esther, it shares with us how Esther came near to the king. She knew that she could find favor and intimacy in the king's presence. It was dangerous to approach the king if not invited. Knowing that she had spent enough intimate moments with him, Esther felt secure enough to approach the king even though she wasn't invited. When you spend quality time with someone, there is an affection that grows within both hearts; which inadvertedly gives you the liberty to enter their presence at any given time. We must pursue the Lord in prayer until we find favor and grace in His presence. In His presence, there is an impartation of anointing and power.

Intercessors need to find Jesus in His bedchamber where He is waiting to show His love and reveal His heart to them. A church that is seeking God in an intimate way is a church that will find satisfaction and joy in knowing that He hears them and will answer them. The confirmation that He hears us when we pray is that He whispers sweet nothings in our ears and confirms His word with signs and wonders.

I dare you to position yourself before the Lord during a time of intense consecration in prayer and let Him pour the oil of His anointing on your thirsty soul, so you can smell the sweet perfume of His presence. I guarantee you that all else will diminish when you taste the pleasantry of His sweet relationship when you abide in His bedchamber.

Don't give up until you press toward Him and experience a deeper intimacy that those who you come in contact with, cannot deny that you have been in His presence.

Chapter Four
Divine Purpose

ost of God's people wander aimlessly through life not knowing their purpose. Now that I'm saved, what is it all about? Why was I chosen to be saved? After sitting in church on Sundays and during weekday services; enjoying the word of God and serving in different capacities in church; going home, to work and then back to church; have you sometimes said to yourself, what is this all about? God saved us to help save others. However, for us to reach our full potential in Him and for us to become an agent of change for the world, we must realize that God has a divine purpose for our lives. But in order for this purpose to be fully activated in our lives, we must get in a birthing position; whereby travailing intercessory prayers can be elicited.

I have mentioned the prayer group earlier that I founded and now serve as Chief Executive Officer, Hannah's Sons and Daughters. This group was organized in 2000. At that time, the name God gave me was Hannah's Daughters. After the men of God were exposed to the great anointing of God's Spirit, they were compelled to join us in seeking the face of God. After seeking God in prayer and seeing Him captivate their spirits to travail with us—*Gird yourselves and lament, you priests; wail, you ministers of the altar…* (Joel 1:13 AMP)—the Lord spoke to me and said, "For the priests are in the house."

What God was saying was that it was time to appoint my husband, Pastor Donald E. Cleveland, Sr., as overseer of Hannah's Daughters Intercessory Prayer Ministry. So, out of obedience to God, I changed the name of the prayer ministry from Hannah's Daughters to Hannah's Sons and Daughters, because the men were now positioning themselves in prayer. God needed a representation and model for them. My husband and I have always worked together closely in ministry, but now God was allowing us to work even more effectively in Hannah's Sons and Daughters Prayer Ministry. In fact, it was Hannah's Daughters that the Lord used to birth our church into existence.

When I started this intercessory prayer ministry, the Lord spoke to me and said, "Many will come pregnant with destiny and purpose, but you will be the one to birth them forth." Some have come knowing their purpose and some, not knowing. But after they positioned themselves to seek God in the birthing of the spirit with travailing prayer, they have come to new dimensions that they themselves did not realize were prevalent in their lives. By obeying God and in seeking His face in prayer, they are now enjoying a purpose-driven life.

When we seek God in intercessory prayer, the only one who gives purpose, He reveals to us our purpose. Sometimes the Lord shows me some of the prayer members' purpose and other times He may not. But if He does, I can only confirm that which is already lying dormant in their spirits.

I'm very leery of people who say that they are prophets, and go around trying to give someone a call that God has not shared with that person. We need to try the spirit to see whether it is of God or not. The Lord will send an unction in your spirit or witness to the word; this is His way of confirming that which is being said. So be very cautious of people who call you to step in an arena that you are not clear about in your spirit. His way will be so plain that a fool will not error.

It is prevalent in our world and in every nation that there is a generation that seems to have no sense of purpose. Even our young men, of every nationality, seem to have no sense of direction and purpose. It is evidently seen with the sagging of the pants, tattoos, piercings on all parts of their bodies, weird and lewd hair cuts, standing on street corners, and having babies by as many women as the notches on their belts. We are the ones who must pass the torch or the mantle to our next generation. We must teach them how to position themselves before God, seek Him until He speaks from Heaven and reveals to them the purpose of their being.

Oddly enough, I find that many people of God do not know what their true purpose is in life. Many try to fulfill their lives by working in every department of the ministry, but they are never fully satisfied. Therefore, after reaching the prime of their lives, they feel empty and unfulfilled. The word says that Jesus came that we might have life and that we might have it more abundantly (John 10:10). How are we going to be able to reach this place of abundance if we don't seek the abundant giver? We must realize that our fulfillment in life is dependent upon our becoming and doing what we were born to be and do. For without purpose, life has no heart.

Ephesians 1:5-6 says, "Having predestinated us unto the adoption of children by Jesus Christ to himself, according to the good pleasure of his will. To the praise of the glory of his grace, wherein he hath made us accepted in the beloved." The Lord has preordained our lives for His purpose. One of the main purposes of His will for our lives is to glorify Him in whatever He has ordained for our lives. The people of God, no matter who they are or where they live, I believe, all want to be successful. Success is being in the perfect will of God.

A person who is purpose-driven will always find a life filled with purpose. When Jesus dwelled on earth, He lived a purpose-filled life. Jesus remained true to His destiny. In John 4:34, Jesus saith unto them, "My meat is to do the will of Him that sent me, and to finish His work." Persecution, betrayal, beatings, nor crucifixion could not separate Him from His divine purpose. Jesus was able to say, "It is finished," after He had endured the agony of the cross. He bowed His head and gave up the ghost (John 19:30).

You must commit your life to pursuing purpose with a passion. God has ordained that man should pray. Luke 18:1 says, "...men ought always to pray, and not to faint..." Saints are fainting because of not knowing their purpose and not having a prayer life. If you are fainting, check to see if your prayer life is in order. God needs you to accept and agree with His will for your life. How are you going to know His purpose for your life if you are not seeking Him in prayer? Travailing prayer will birth God's divine purpose for your life. Establish a time with God and seek Him for His will for your life. Don't give up until He speaks and reveals to you His purpose for your life. Then stay before Him until He gives complete directions of how to implement the blueprint that He has revealed to you.

In this last hour the Lord is going to gather His intercessors from every corner of the earth. This glory is going to be released upon a Joshua generation. Joshua was "armed and dangerous" and his proclamation rung throughout Israel when he stated, "Who's on the Lord's side?" He had his sword drawn and he was ready for war. Intercessors, it is time to stand up and be counted in this new millennium and seek God with fasting and praying until He births His latter rain upon this earth. When we cry out to God with intense intercessory prayer, He will send His glory amongst His people and they will comprehend their purpose and take it by storm.

FRANCES CLEVELAND

Chapter Five

The Power Of Prayer and Intercession

...The earnest (heart-felt, continued) prayer of a righteous man makes tremendous power available [dynamic in its working].

James 5:16 AMP

Prayer is fellowshipping with the Father—a vital, personal contact with God, who is more than enough. We are to be in constant communion with Him:

For the eyes of the Lord are upon the righteous [those who are upright and in right standing with God], and His ears are attentive (open) to their prayer...

1 Peter 3:12 AMP

Prayer is not to be a religious form with no power. It is to be effective and accurate, bringing results. God watches over His Word to perform it. (Jer. 1:12) Prayer that brings results must be based on God's Word.

For the Word that God speaks is alive and full of power [making it active, operative, energizing and effective]; it is sharper than any two-edged sword, penetrating to the dividing line of the breath of life (soul) and (the immortal) spirit, and of joints and marrow [of the deepest parts of our nature], exposing and sifting and analyzing and judging the very thoughts and purposes of the heart.

Hebrews 4:12 AMP

God did not leave us without His thoughts and His ways for we have His Word—His bond. God instructs us to call Him and He will answer and show us great and mighty things. (Jer. 33:3) Prayer is to be exciting – not drudgery.

It takes persistence—someone who is determined and relentlessly seeking the face of God. As we pray in faith, God moves, knowing that all things, whatsoever we ask in prayer, believing, we shall receive them (Matt. 21:22).

God says that His eyes run to and fro throughout the whole earth to show Himself strong on the behalf of those whose hearts are blameless toward Him (2 Chron. 16:9). He tells us to come boldly to the throne of grace to obtain mercy and find grace to help in time of need (appropriate and well-timed help).

> *Prayer must be the foundation of every Christian endeavor. Any failure is a prayer failure.*

The prayer armor is for every believer, every member of the Body of Christ, who will put it on and walk in it. For the weapons of our warfare are not carnal, but mighty through God for the pulling down of strongholds of the enemy (Satan, the god of this world, and all his demonic forces). Spiritual warfare takes place in prayer (2 Cor. 10:4, Eph. 6:12, 18).

There are many different kinds of prayers, such as the prayer of thanksgiving and praise, the prayer of dedication and worship, and the prayer that changes things. All prayer involves a time of fellowship with the Father.

In 1 Timothy 2, we are admonished and urged that petitions, prayers, intercessions and thanksgiving be offered on behalf of all men (1 Tim. 2:1 AMP). Prayer is our responsibility.

Prayer must be the foundation of every Christian endeavor. Any failure is a prayer failure. We are not to be ignorant concerning God's Word. God desires for His people to be successful. To be filled with a full, deep, and clear knowledge of His will (His Word), and to bear fruit in every good work (Col. 1:9-13); which brings honor and glory to Him (John 15:8). He desires that we know how to pray, for the prayer of the upright is His delight (Prov. 15:8). He has given us the Holy Spirit to help our infirmities when we know not how to pray as we ought (Rom. 8:26).

Important: Prayer does not cause faith to work, but faith causes prayer to work. Therefore, any prayer problem is a problem of doubt—doubting the integrity of the Word and the ability of God to stand behind His promises or the statements of fact in the Word.

We can spend fruitless hours in prayer if our hearts are not prepared beforehand. Preparation of the heart and the spirit comes from meditation in His Word. Meditation on who we are in Christ, what He is to us, and what the Holy Spirit can mean to us as we become God-inside minded.

When we use God's Word in prayer it should not be done from a careless or contempt attitude. Rather it should be done from a platform of obedience and full understanding of what is taking place in the spirit. But do not be mistaken. There is nothing "magical" nor "manipulative" about it. No set pattern or device in order to satisfy what we want, or desire out of our flesh. Instead we are holding God's Word before Him. We are confessing what He says belongs to us.

We expect His divine intervention while we choose not to look at the things that are seen but at the things that are unseen, for the things that are seen are subject to change (2 Cor. 4:18).

It is not just saying prayers that get results, but it is spending time with the Father (learning His wisdom, drawing on His strength, being filled with His quietness, and basking in His love) that brings results to our prayers. Praise the Lord!

FRANCES CLEVELAND

Chapter Six

Prayer Components

Prayer is basically made up of these elements:

- Praise
- Forgiveness
- Confession
- Petition
- Intercession
- Reading the Bible
- Meditation
- Thanksgiving
- Praying the Word
- Singing
- Listening

All of the things that I have listed above are very general. When we talk about prayer, we must understand that prayer is a vast subject.

Therefore, there are many more aspects to it than this list suggest. However, you will find that when on prays, his prayer will almost always be comprised of these elements. If you learn them and use them in your prayers, it will give you an understanding of what you are to do when praying. As you practice prayer, it will become easier and your prayer time will be a joy rather than a dreaded frustration.

Praise

We enter into prayer through the door of praise and worship. We should also conclude every prayer session with praise and worship. So when we do this as a conclusion, we exalt the nature of God. Jesus emphasized this when He taught His disciples to pray. Notice the suggested closing, "…For thine is the kingdom, and the power, and the glory, forever. Amen" (Matt. 6:13). Your pray life should never be so structured that you do not relax and allow the Spirit to lead you. Intercession, for example, can rarely be done in five minutes. It would not be unusual to spend an entire hour in praise or intercession as the Spirit directs.

Forgiveness

Matthew 6:12 says, "And forgive us our debts, as we forgive our debtors." Unforgiveness will hinder your prayers before the Lord. We have some faults within areas of our lives where there is lack and immaturity that we haven't conquered. Colossians 3:13 speaks of this, "Forbearing one another, and forgiving one another, if any man have a quarrel against any: even as Christ forgave you, so also do ye." Also in Matthew 6:14-15, Jesus says, "For if ye forgive men their trespasses, your heavenly Father will also forgive you. But if ye forgive not men their trespasses, neither will your Father forgive your trespasses."

Before we ask God for anything we should always ask Him to search our hearts, making sure that there is no unforgiveness in our spirit.

Confession

Confession is the act of making known one's faults or sins. There is an old cliché that says, "Confession is good for the soul." Before we come before God, we should first humble ourselves, and wait on Him to see whether He reveals some unconfessed sin in our lives. Always remember that the only way to have an audience with our God and King is to confess our faults or sins. Because no man knows his heart, it is exceedingly wicked. It is not in man to direct his steps. The Lord orders our steps. Confession will bring healing to the one who humbles him or her self before Him. James 5:16 says, "Confess your faults one to another, and pray one for another, that ye may be healed. The effectual fervent prayer of a righteous man availeth much." "If we confess our sins, he is faithful and just to forgive us of our sins, and to cleanse us from all unrighteousness." (I John 1:9)

Petition

The word petition is an earnest request or prayer. There was a joy that flooded my soul when I realized that I could come boldly before my Lord's throne and earnestly request anything according to His Word. I John 5:14-15 says, "And this is the confidence that we have in him, that, if we ask any thing according to his will, he heareth us: And if we know that he hear us, whatsoever we ask, we know that we have the petitions that we desired of him."

Intercession

Center your prayers in intercession for the LOST and the dying world. Make a list of those you want to pray for daily. Intercession is praying for the lost; which is the most intense dimension of prayer.

You can expect the power of God to be released through this form of prayer. Intercession is love: God's love flowing through us. Intercession is the crying of the heart for souls. God has mysteriously made Himself dependent upon our prayers. Whereas petition involves things, intercession involves souls. Intercession is working with God in the job of redeeming others. In this work as in others, "…we are laborers together with God…" (1 Cor. 3:9).

Read the Bible

It may surprise you to hear the suggestion that you should read your Bible during prayer. However, the Word is enlightening to the eyes (Ps. 19:9). When you read the Bible, new possibilities are made clear. Although prayer time must not become study time, a brief moment of scripture is vital to complete prayer.

Meditation

When one meditates on God, his mind is very active. In meditation you ponder on the spiritual things of God's Word and Spirit. Note, God's Word to Joshua, "This book of the law shall not depart out of thy mouth; but thou shalt meditate therein day and night, that thou mayest observe to do according to all that is written therein: for then thou shalt make thy way prosperous, and then thou shalt have good success." (Jos. 1:8)

Thanksgiving

Psalm 100:4 says, "Enter into his gates with thanksgiving and into his courts with praise: be thankful unto him, and bless his name." We should always enter the gates of prayer with thanksgiving, and before his presence with praise. Thanksgiving is the act of giving thanks. It is the state of the heart. A heart that is full of appreciation toward someone (God). Oh give thanks unto the Lord for all He has done.

He has done great things for us. If you are grateful in your heart toward God's greatness, there will always be an outward manifestation of thanksgiving that will exude from your spirit. His presence will overshadow you and many will know that you have been alone with Him. Let the spirit of thanksgiving flow in every phase of your prayer.

Praying the Word

In Matthew 24:35, the words of Jesus say that Heaven and earth shall pass away, but my words shall not pass away. The word of the Lord will last forever. All else will fail, but God's Word has proven to be true. God recognizes His Word in prayer and hastens to perform it. God's Word will not return unto Him void, but it will accomplish that which He has sent it forth to do. So praying God's Word will empower your prayer life and bring you into alignment of His will and purpose. We can't manipulate God and try to bring our own philosophy and will in prayer because He will not hear us. He watches over His Word to perform it. If we have confidence that He hears us, we can ask whatsoever, according to His Word, and He will grant our petitions.

Singing

Psalm 100:1-2 says, "Make a joyful noise unto the Lord, all ye lands. Serve the Lord with gladness: come before his presence with singing." Sometimes people, who have a melodious voice, love to sing to their lovers at their wedding ceremony. So as it is in the natural, it is also in the spirit. When we accept the Lord as our personal Savior, we become married to Him, and should make melody of songs unto Him. Jesus is our lover and there is an intimacy that exudes from our spirits when we sing to God in prayer. When we are excited, and full of praise, we will lavish Him with extravagant worship and singing for all He has done. In 1 Corinthians 14:15, Paul states that he will pray with the spirit and he will pray with the understanding also: He will sing with the spirit, and He will sing with the understanding also. Let's sing unto the Lord a new song.

Listening

Prayer is not all talking to God, it involves listening also. Listening, for many, is a lost art. However, in our prayers, we must establish good listening habits. God speaks in the still small voice (1 Kings 19:11-12) to those who pray. Remember, listening is different from meditation. When we listen, we receive direct orders from God's Spirit. Make certain that your praying includes listening

Chapter Seven
The Watchman Anointing

Never in the time of history have we as the 21st century saints been under an attack of the enemy to succumb to a place of apathy and complacency in the spirit than now. These are perilous times and we need God to impart unto us a watchful spirit. The enemy is constantly attacking the saints and finding ways to take our focus off of God. At the hour of Jesus being offered up for crucifixion, He told His disciples that "His soul was exceedingly sorrowful, even unto death; tarry ye here, and watch with me."

After seeing that the spirit was willing, but the flesh was weak, He asked them with amazement, "What, could ye not watch with me one hour?" Then He said, "Watch and pray, that ye enter not into temptation." (Matt. 26:40-41)

We are called to be watchmen in the body of Christ. A watchman is someone who keeps things, places and individuals safe. They ensure against loss, theft or damage. They keep things intact. They are a guard-keeper. The watchman guards and protects an individual from danger and harm. They are shields—secret service agents of the kingdom, guarding and watching over others. The watchman is a representation of Jesus Christ in watching others. They have the innate ability to discern the attack of the enemy. The Lord has equipped them for spiritual warfare. They are alert and sensitive to the wiles of Satan.

The watchman walks in prophetic intercession. Watchmen, also gatekeepers, would watch from the wall of the cities for two things: enemies and messengers. They were assigned to watch for messengers to inform the gatekeepers about when to open the gates and when not to. They were responsible for sending out a midnight cry. In Isaiah 21:11, Dumah cried unto Isaiah and asked him, "Watchman what of the night? Watchman what of the night?" The Lord will give the watchman a word concerning dark times in our nation and they will cry before it comes. In the days of old there were runners who were responsible for carrying messages from city to city, and they would cry out when there was a friendly messenger approaching. Qualified and skilled watchmen could often recognize the runners by their stride before ever seeing their faces.

Here are some basic scriptures concerning being watchful unto prayer.

- Ephesians 6:18
- II Corinthians 2:11
- Genesis 2:15
- II Kings 6:8-16
- Isaiah 21:6-8
- Jeremiah 51:12
- Isaiah 62:6
- Luke 21:36
- Mark 14:34, 38
- I Peter 5:8
- I Corinthians 16:13
- Isaiah 21:11-12

FRANCES CLEVELAND

Chapter Eight
Most Frequently Asked Questions About Prayer and Intercession

We are to pray "for the pardon of sin, for the Holy Spirit, for a Christ like temper, for wisdom and strength to do His work, for any gift that He has promised, we may ask: Then we are to believe that we receive, and return thanks to God that we have received."

1. What is the Scripture injunction in regard to prayer?

I will therefore that men pray everywhere, lifting up holy hands, without wrath and doubting.   1 Tim. 2:8

2. How does the Savior illustrate the willingness of Heaven to grant favors to those who ask?

If ye then, being evil, know how to give good gifts unto your children, how much more shall your Father which is in heaven give good things to them that ask him? Matt. 7:11

3. Why is it necessary to ask God for all these things?

Every good gift and every perfect gift is from above, and cometh down from the Father of lights, with whom is no variableness, neither shadow of turning." James 1:17

Note: From this text some may be led to question the utility of power, the Father does not change. "Why, then, one may ask, try to change His mind by our prayers?" It is true that praying to God does not change His mind in the least; that is not the design of prayer. It is the petitioner who is to be benefited by His prayer. God is ever ready to bestow on His children the blessings they need. His sending Christ to die for the world without any request from man, shows His willingness to help. He also says that He is not willing that any should perish (2 Peter 3:9). Now, when any one feels His need of help to that extent that he is willing to acknowledge his sins, and his lost condition without God; then the Lord lets that individual have the blessing that had been held up all his life, and that God was not only willing, but anxious to give him. God's mind is not, therefore, changed in the least; but the petitioner must be changed. Otherwise the bestowal of blessings would serve to keep him away from God and defeat the very object that was in view sending Christ to die for the world. The object, therefore, of prayer, is to cause the sinner to realize his needs and to feel that he must perish unless they are supplied. This could not be so, if one had all he needed without asking.

4. How should we pray to God?

I will pray with the spirit, and I will pray with the understanding also. 1 Cor. 14:15. This implies meditation and examination of one's life.

5. With what should the prayers of a suppliant be mingled?

Be careful for nothing; but in everything by prayer and supplication, with thanksgiving let your requests be made known unto God. Phil. 4:6

6. What must precede our petitions to please God?

But without faith it is impossible to please him; for he that cometh to God must believe that he is, and that he is a rewarder of them that diligently seek him. Heb. 11:6

7. How strong must this faith be?

Therefore I say unto you, what things soever ye desire, when ye pray, believe that ye receive them, and ye shall have them. Mark 11:24. This is when one prays for that which he needs and trust God implicitly that he has no doubt his petition has been, in effect, answered; and therefore, he will have no more anxiety over the matter, but trust it wholly with God, as a case committed to Him

8. When praying for forgiveness, how should we feel toward those who have in any way injured us?

And when ye stand praying, forgive if ye have aught against any; that your Father also which is in heaven may forgive you your trespasses. Mark 11:25

9. How often does the apostle exhort the church to pray?

Praying always with all prayer and supplication in the Spirit. Eph. 6:18

10. How does he express himself on this point elsewhere?

Pray without ceasing. 1 Thess 5:17

11. In the parable of the importunate widow, what reason did the judge give for finally heeding her petition?

Though I fear not God, nor regard man; yet because this widow troubleth me, I will avenge her, lest by her continual coming she weary me. Luke 18:4, 5

12. How does the Savior apply the parable?

And the Lord said, Hear what the unjust judge saith. And shall not God avenge his own elect, which cry day and night unto him, though he bear long with them? Luke 18:6, 7.

13. What is required on our part if we are kept from our foes?

Watch and pray, that ye enter not into temptation: the spirit indeed is willing, but the flesh is weak. Matt. 26:41.

14. On what occasions did David receive strength and encouragement?

When I remember thee upon my bed, and meditate on thee in the nightwatches. Ps. 63:6

15. What did he say of the man who was truly blessed?

His delight is in the law of the Lord; and in his law doth he meditate day and night. Ps. 1:2

16. Will such a condition of mind be distasteful to one who really loves God?

My meditation of him shall be sweet. Ps. 104:34

17. What is the special duty of those who live in the time when the Lord's coming is expected?

Take ye heed, watch and pray: for ye know not when the time is... Watch ye therefore: for ye know not when the master of the house cometh, as even, or at midnight, or at the cockcrowing, or in the morning: lest coming suddenly he find you sleeping. And what I say unto you I say unto all. Watch. Mark 13:33-37

18. As the Lord's coming draws near, what will make the duty of prayer and watchfulness more imperative?

Woe to the inhabiters of the earth and of the sea! For the devil is come down unto you, having great wrath, because he knoweth that he hath but a short time. Rev. 12:12

19. Can we at that time have all the help we desire to withstand our enemies?

Verily, verily, I say unto you, whatsoever ye shall ask the Father in my name, he will give it to you. John 16:23.

20. If help does not come when it is first asked, what should one do?

And shall not God avenge his own elect, which cry day and night unto him, though he bear long with them? I tell you that he will avenge them speedily. Luke 18:7, 8. Wait on the Lord: be of good courage, and he shall strengthen thine heart: wait, I say, on the Lord. Ps. 27:14

21. What blessed promise is granted to those who are found watching when the Lord comes?

Blessed are those servants, whom the lord when he cometh shall find watching: verily I say unto you, that he shall gird himself, and make them to sit down to meat, and will come forth and serve them. Luke 12:37

22. What must accompany faith in order that our hearts shall not condemn us, and that we may have the things for which we ask?

And whatsoever we ask, we receive of him, because we keep his commandments, and do those things that are pleasing in His sight. I John 3:22

Note: If condemnation (a knowledge of guilt) rests on an individual, he has no confidence when before God, a lack of which forbids an answer to prayer. But the last quoted verse says that what we receive in answer to our petitions is because we are obedient to the commandments, which proves conclusively that without such obedience, one cannot exercise that faith which will bring answers to prayer; for faith without works is dead, being alone.

23. If one does not ask in faith, what does he gain?

But let him ask in faith, nothing wavering: for he that wavereth is like a wave of the sea, driven with the wind and tossed. For let not that man think that he shall receive anything of the Lord. James 1:6, 7

Personal

Prayer

Testimonies

By Margie Haskin

When I first started coming to Hannah's Sons and Daughters prayer on Monday nights, my sister who lives in Florida would listen by cell phone for as long as the signal would last. One particular night of prayer, Prophetess Cleveland began to earnestly go into prayer against cancer demons.

My sister, at that time, felt led of God to have a breast exam done. Unfortunately, she found a lump in her breast. The next few weeks we went through the gruesome process of waiting on God to reveal Himself. On her first visit to the doctor's office, they confirmed what we were praying against. They did not want to take any chances on it spreading and recommended that she have it removed. When she went back to take x-rays again, only by the grace and mercy of God, the lump was gone.

One Monday night the Lord spoke to Prophetess Cleveland concerning a $50.00 offering from five people. I was one of the five that stood in faith. My son Maurice is in a discipleship program, and at that time the tuition was $2000 in arrears. This negative balance would determine whether my son would be able to graduate to the next level in the program; which was in June, and whether or not he would be welcomed back in order to finish it. Wednesday morning, after I planted the $50 seed, I received a phone call from my son stating that he had an anonymous donation of $1000.00 given towards his tuition. Also, God blessed me with the remaining $1000.00, and now his tuition is paid in full. Glory be to our God, He has proven Himself faithful again.

Also, another Monday night my niece, Tesha, came with me to prayer. She stated that after Prophetess Cleveland laid hands on her, she felt the power of God surge through her entire body. She said it had been a long time since she felt God's peace on her in that way and knew after that night she would never be the same again. That night she felt so much peace after she left. Now, her relationship with God has sky-rocketed as well as become more intimate.

Since coming to Hannah's Sons and Daughters Prayer Ministry and planting seeds into the ministry, there is a constant flow of money that comes into my life. I made a commitment to either sow $300.00 to the ministry and/or sell 10 tickets @ $30.00 each for a program the ministry was sponsoring.

I knew that I did not have $300.00, so I prayed and asked God to help me. His faithfulness was proven again. All of my tickets were sold.

By Janice Sims

My first experience with Hannah's Sons and Daughters prayer was in November 2004, when I first heard about Prophetess Frances Cleveland's prayer, as they called it. I came once with a friend who told me about the prayer, and that was it. I told some of my associates, "This is where you will find me from now on, on Monday nights."

I had never experienced prayer like this before. It was an awesome experience. I had also heard about the 5 a.m. prayer the 2nd week of every month, but to be truthful, I didn't want to get up that early in the morning.

But I had a hunger that I couldn't explain. I was so dissatisfied. I was about to have a fit. I was already a member of a very large church, being taught and fed very well. I attended Bible study, was very active in the choir, and when the doors opened, you could find me there. Even when we held services on Saturday nights, I was there. But after a while, church as usual didn't work for me anymore. I felt like something was missing and knew I had to have more. I would go to church, get a good word, but I would still have this hunger inside of me. At that time I didn't know it was intercessory prayer that I was longing for within.

After church, members would be saying, "Didn't he preach?, or "Wasn't that a good word!" All I could say was yeah! But I knew I needed more than what I was getting. I didn't know at that time what it was. So I told the Lord, "Lord you've got to give me directions, instructions or manifest your word." So the Lord instructed me to set my alarm clock and attend 5 a.m. prayer everyday in February 2005, including Saturdays. This is what I was hungry for, prayer. Prayer fulfilled me, satisfied me and it was the missing part in my life. I finally found the place where I belonged. I was called to be an intercessor.

I had such a hunger for God that once I had been introduced to Hannah's Sons and Daughters Prayer Ministry, I couldn't wait for Monday to come around again so that I could attend prayer. I found myself just rushing for Monday nights to come. So I had to learn how to calm myself down and learn to enjoy each day, one day at a time. That's why the prayer on every Saturday was such a blessing to my thirsty soul.

Since coming to prayer, the Lord had me to move my membership to Breaking of Day Family Church. I wasn't looking for a church home when I came; I only came because I heard about the prayer. I was already a member of a Mega Church, but God set me up real good and I truly thank Him for it. I have been so blessed since being a part of Hannah's Sons and Daughters Prayer Ministry. I can never go back to where I was. I am such a changed person. I thank God for Prophetess Cleveland and Apostle Cleveland. God Bless.

Also since I started with Hannah's Sons and Daughters Prayer Ministry, my youngest son has started going to church again, paying his tithes and he has begun to seek the Lord in prayer. Now, the Lord is using him on his job to evangelize to his co-workers.

I have such a love for Prophetess Cleveland that I have never experienced before. So I had to ask the Lord, "Why do I love her so much?" And the Lord let me know, it is because she is my spiritual mother. I've never had a spiritual mother before and I truly thank God for you, First Lady Cleveland.

For just being you, for the sacrifices you have made, for your obedience and for everything you've given up in order for you to be my spiritual mom and to many others.

I love you

By Pernail Freeman

Giving all thanks and praises to God, who is the head of my life. I thank God for blessing me to be a part of Hannah's Sons and Daughters Prayer Ministry. A good friend, Shelley Webb, invited me to this dynamic intercessory prayer ministry about five years ago.

When I came to Hannah's Sons and Daughters Intercessory prayer, my spirit was crushed beyond measure. I had lost my mother to cancer after having a three year battle with it.

I was searching for peace of mind; which I hadn't had for such a long time. I knew God was a healer and restorer, but my light had become somewhat dim from battling with so much hurt. I had a lot of anger and frustration that had been lying dormant in my life for many years. It was easy to cover up the hurt and disappointment, so it became a way of life for me. But there was a hunger for something more in my life.

Little did I know that Hannah's Sons and Daughters intercessory prayer would hold all the answers to my freedom from bondage.

I asked God to order my footsteps and I became a member of not only Hannah's Sons and Daughters, but also Breaking of Day Family Church.

The road I have been traveling on has had many potholes and in some cases avalanches, but every obstacle course has lead me to the feet of God crying out for His new grace, mercy and direction. God has used Prophetess Frances Cleveland to help me understand that no situations are impossible with God.

When I want to crawl into my cave away from everyone, she prays for me. You better be ready when she prays for you. The heat that generates from just one of Mother Cleveland's prayers is coming into that cave to bring you out with your hands up. And when you come out, she is waiting with open arms to wrap you up in her unfailing love. She has taught me how to go beyond the veil and to push until something happens. We are becoming little spiritual prayer giants.

Because Prophetess Cleveland cared enough to obey the will of God, and to gather the women and men from the north, south, east and the west, we all are challenged to wail. I don't know where I would be today without her. I can now see down the road to my destiny and the vision becomes clearer and clearer every time I go down on my knees in prayer.

Because of the prayer and teaching ministry, when everything looks grey, I know how to pray until there is a break in the clouds of my life. I have been blessed with what my soul has been searching for all my life. I remember when there was a time I thought suicide was the best way out of the depression, heartache and disappointment I was experiencing. But God stepped in and gave me a brighter tomorrow and here I am.

Some days are hard, but the word of God says "the steps of a good man are ordered by the Lord."

I thank God from the bottom of my heart for Prophetess Frances Cleveland (a.k.a Mother Cleveland to her daughters in the gospel). You are truly a Proverbs 31 Woman.

Proverbs 31:28 says, "Her children arise up, and call her blessed; her husband also, and he praiseth her."

You are teaching your sons and daughters how to build up the kingdom of God through the power of intercessory prayer. Mighty intercessory warriors are being birthed from your travailing before the altar of God. And I thank God that I am one of them.

Your daughter forever.

By Tracy McDougal

*G*reetings in the name of our Lord and Savior, Jesus Christ. Prophetess Cleveland I do not even know where to begin. I remember when I first moved to Dallas, Texas, you were one of the first speakers that I had the privilege to hear. I was in amazement as to how dynamically God used you. It was so anointed and powerful it seemed too great to be real. God made a divine connection between you and I even then. I remember the first time you ever declared prophecy over my life and you saw the destiny that God had placed upon me. Over the four years that I lived in Dallas, Texas. You continued to push me forward into that destiny. You have been a midwife of the spirit, helping me to give birth to the spiritual babies that God has given me. You are always encouraging the women of God and assuring us that we are not to be stagnated in our walk with God.

I have made myself a part of Hannah's Sons and Daughters. I love you all so much. I admire the women and men of your organization. Prophetess Cleveland you have instilled greatness in the women just by the example that you are. When people in a ministry (all of them) present themselves (dress, conversation, lifestyle, prayer life) as such awesome women and men of God, one must stop and assess where is such behavior learned? You are such a true example of a woman after God's own heart. And it is respected both near and far.

Monday night prayer made such a difference in my spiritual life. I began to come to prayer and messed around and got myself addicted to prayer! Through your travailing and weeping, you have given to many prayer warriors. I don't think you really understand the degree of how you have changed lives spiritually and socially.

When I moved back to North Carolina in March 2005, I continued in intercessory prayer at my local church. I found myself leading the prayer many times and ushering in the spirit of God. God was using me and I did not even realize that I could be used in such a way.

Prophetess Cleveland, the seeds that you planted were present when I was in Dallas, Texas, but God needed them to flourish in Durham, North, Carolina. I thank God for the divine connection that He made between us.

In intercessory prayer a couple of things have been prophesied to me here in NC. I would like to share them with you because it's your teaching and training as a prayer warrior that impacted my life in such a way.

I have an Old Testament anointing. God shows me visions and people's spirits, so I would know what to intercede for daily. When I pray peace, calmness enters into the room. When I worship, it is like Heaven falls upon us. I am an atmosphere setter.

I wanted to share that little bit with you because it's through learning how to travail and weep before God that all of these things are possible.

No one can sit under all of that anointing in Hannah's Sons and Daughters prayer and not somehow be impacted. It has really changed my life. I am so eager to please God and to do the will of my Heavenly Father.

I am on fire for God. I have really been blessed through your ministry and your prayers. You and Pastor Cleveland are one of a kind. I mean that!

I love you guys so much and everybody in your church. They have such a loving spirit about them, just like their leaders.

You have the victory and the devil is defeated in the name of Jesus. Every desire that you have, God is going to bring it to pass. Glory to God! God says to you on this day, even your thoughts, He's going to bless!

You are blessed in the city and blessed in the field. You are blessed in your rising up and in your down sitting, blessed in your coming in and in your going out.

You are more than a conqueror!

Love You Much!!

By First Lady Gina Smith

Hannah's Sons and Daughters Intercessory Prayer Ministry has truly blessed my family, our church and me. I would not be as effective in prayer today if it were not for God using Prophetess Frances Cleveland in teaching, training and instructing in apostolic and prophetic intercessory prayer.

God was dealing with me many years about being an intercessor; I had a passion for prayer. So, I read several books on intercessory prayer. I had even joined a women's prayer group. However, I still yearned for more. Then I went to a prayer clinic and I picked up a book, written by a collaboration of authors.

There was a chapter written by Prophetess Cleveland talking about the different stages you will go through in birthing an intercessory prayer group. What she wrote captivated me so much that I had to find Hannah's Sons and Daughters Intercessory Prayer Ministry. I found out that the ministry had prayer on Monday nights, and was located in Dallas, Texas. Then I went on the Internet and found Prophetess Cleveland and called for directions to the ministry. I came to prayer that following Monday night and now it has been a year. It has totally changed the way I pray.

I have learned so much that I could write on and on. One thing I can say, I had to learn that I must be skilled to see in the spirit, to know how to maneuver around the enemy. The Bible speaks of God's people perishing from the lack of knowledge. I was much unlearned in the area of apostolic and prophetic intercessory prayer. Now, I understand what God has called me to do in intercessory prayer. My soul is so delighted that I am able to please the Father for what He has called me to do in intercessory prayer. I encourage anyone who wants to take their prayer life to deeper depths and wants to sharpen their skills in prayer to come to Hannah's Sons and Daughters. Our world needs more men and women intercessors, armed and dangerous, to pull down Satan's kingdom.

By Chanattra Booker

I went to prayer about two weeks ago and Prophetess Cleveland said get a picture in your mind of what you want God to do, and believe it. So I shouted like I had received what I believed God to give me during prayer.

The next day, I received a call from the Mortgage Company saying I could move into my new home. I was believing God for a new home.

Hannah's Sons and Daughters prayer has been such an encouragement to me. When I was about to give up and the enemy was trying to take my life, God had a way of escape for me while I was coming to prayer.

I thank God for all that He has done for me through this prayer ministry. My life will never be the same.

I thank God for my life, having peace in my mind and for First Lady Cleveland.

By Elder Clifford Bryant Sr.

I first heard about Hannah's Sons and Daughters prayer back in February 2004, through barber shop talk. After a couple of months of hearing repeated testimonies about the move of God in these prayer services, where people of all walks of life and denominations were being blessed, I decided to investigate for myself. Being a man of God and needing a miracle in my life, I went with great expectation. Entering the prayer service as a curious back seat observer, I kneeled down on my knees to pray, as it seemed customary.

After about 5 to 10 minutes I rose to my seat only to notice I was the only one up. As I sat waiting for others to get up off their knees from praying, it didn't appear that they would be getting off their knees anytime soon. So back on my knees I went.

After 15 to 20 minutes of prayer, I rose again to find that once again only I had rose. I was told the intercessory prayer service lasted about one and a half to two hours and that many times the spirit of God would then move prophetically by the one in charge usually none other than its founder, Prophetess Frances Cleveland.

Nevertheless, I went back on my knees a third time. After another 15 to 20 minutes of sincere prayer, I was wise enough at this time to stick my head up to see if anyone had rose, not so. I begin to understand that it was meant (literally) on your knees or face for nearly two hours crying out to the Father with sweat and tears in true intercessory corporate prayer.

A body of saints followed the leader in crying out in prayer for the nations of the world, global and national government leaders, local county and city officials. A series of prayers continued for pastors and missionaries around the world, rebuking sin from Hollywood to our nation's capital. Intense prayer continued for the healing of nations, broken marriages, tearing down strongholds and binding up devils and loosing blessings on God's people. You name it, this prayer group prayed for it.

I continued visiting these services for a few weeks because I quickly noticed that it was making a difference in my life. Being a prayer warrior myself, I understood the benefits of fasting and prayer. Speaking of fasting, this is one of the prerequisites of this weekly Monday night prayer group that I quickly grew to appreciate, and that is to fast from Sunday mid-night to 3pm Monday.

Following this fasting procedure each week, one would notice that when coming to 7:00 p.m. prayer, the battle was nearly won. Meaning you didn't have to work or push so hard in prayer for the victory because of pre-fasting.

After understanding that praying for an hour and a half meant just that and attending for several weeks, on March 19th 2004 a word from the Lord came to me through His prophetess, and a timely word it was.

Then another word on May 10th, and another on June 7th, and another on June 14th, and another on September 12th, I could go on.

You see I document every word that the Lord has given me for I believe God will do what He said He would do. And He hasn't failed me, yet, and He won't.

7 Surely the Lord GOD will do nothing, but he revealeth his secret unto his servants the prophets.

Amos 3:7 (KJV)

As I close this testimony, let me backup a couple of months. On June 20th 2004, I was in Florida on vacation. While attending a service there a word from the Lord came to me through His prophet saying "God wants you to move your (family) membership to a smaller church, pay no attention to its size, for the need to be met in your family requires special attention from the pastors of a smaller setting....etc."

After prayer and seeking God on this matter, it didn't take me to be a rocket scientist to know that the Holy Spirit was leading my family and me to Breaking of Day Family Church, headquarters of Hannah's Sons and Daughters.

My wife, who had not yet visited Breaking of Day Family Church or one of the Hannah's Sons and Daughters prayer services, wasn't to quick to agree, but wanted to visit other churches (meaning shop around). However, after one visit to Breaking of Day Family Church, she without a doubt was totally convinced that this is where God wanted us to be. Glory! The rest is history. Our life was never the same. With the storms and trials, which lied ahead for us, God knew where we needed to be to ride out the storm.

I can sum up this testimony with two verses of scripture

14 If my people, which are called by my name, shall humble themselves, and pray, and seek my face, and turn from their wicked ways; then will I hear from heaven, and will forgive their sin, and will heal their land.

¹⁵ Now mine eyes shall be open, and mine ears attend unto the prayer *that is made* in this place.

2 Chron. 7:14-15 (KJV)

By Jacqueline Owens

I give honor to God for giving Prophetess Frances Cleveland the vision to call the daughters of Zion back to the altars of prayer, and to raise up a united group of men and women intercessors willing to travail for the birth of a mighty move of God. Hannah's Sons and Daughters has impacted my life in so many ways. Yolanda Morgan, an angel from God invited me to Monday night prayer and this is where it all began.

I knew that night that my life would never be the same. I was going through some difficult times and really didn't know how to handle my tests, but I did know I needed something and that something was a fresh anointing of the Holy Ghost and this place had it. It's been three and a half years with Hannah's Sons and Daughters and I realize now why God would wake me up in the middle of the night to pray. God was stirring up my gifts, but I didn't understand what was going on.

I just found myself running to prayer every Monday night. I learned to cry out for others and not focus on my situations. I didn't realize how intercession through travailing was such a deep part of me until recently when I became apart of a conference prayer line and I would find myself travailing, moaning, and groaning during the call.

Prophetess Cleveland's ministry has helped me to answer the call in fulfilling my purpose and has imparted the spirit of intercession through travailing so that I can use this gift for the building of the kingdom.

Your Daughter in Zion

By Janice Cleveland

When the Lord was calling me to Hannah's Sons and Daughters prayer, my flesh did not see the real need for such prayer. As I began to come out of so called disobedience, God started to tug at my spirit to come up to a closer and higher place in Him. I went through a period of breaking. There were just some things I wanted to hold on to, that held me captive, and I wanted to do things my own way.

I was raised in a home where my mother was a prayer warrior; it was infused in me. The devil fought me with "tooth and nail" for my prayer life—from depression and oppression, to struggles in my mind. As I began to position myself in prayer, these spirits were rebuked. I went back and forth with God about prayer. I couldn't believe that all I needed to do, was obey God and let Him use me in prayer.

I did not learn how to intercede for others and this nation until I submitted myself to Hannah's Sons and Daughters prayer. It brought me from haughtiness to humility. Now, I realize that I can't do without this prayer. God has showed me that the corporate anointing that dwells amongst this prayer group keeps demons in my home, mind, finances and marriage at bay.

In this phase of my life, May 23, 2005, I am elevated in my mentality. I know because of the destiny upon my life as well as my husband's life. The fight is going to be great, but the word of God proclaims that the effectual fervent prayer of the righteous availeth much. Only a prayer of travail and intercession of this magnitude could have brought my family and me out of the very clutches of Satan. Praise God for the victory. Thanks to God for Hannah's Sons and Daughters, for it has caused me to triumph.

The woman of God that is being used in this hour constantly pushed me, even when I recoiled, she knew her place was to help shape and mold me. The anointing and deliverance ministry that she carries has played a very vital part of my survival. Oh, where would I be without the power that this woman of God possesses?

Thank you, Mother Frances M. Cleveland, for dying to yourself to see me live.

Appendix I

Vision Statement

This ministry has been ordained and established by God in this generation to call the people of God back to the altars of prayer; and to raise up a united group of intercessors willing to travail for the birth of a mighty move of God and fresh anointing of the Holy Ghost in this final hour.

We have been called to the Kingdom for such a time as this, who will consecrate ourselves in fasting and prayer as mighty warriors under the hand of the Lord. That we might stand in the gap against the forces of the enemy and wrought deliverance for those held in bondage. And who will, through the power of prayer and faith in God's Word, impact the world and change the course of nations so that His glory may cover the earth.

Appendix II
Ministry Objectives

Provoke an intense hunger and thirst for greater intimacy with God.

Train and equip the people of God to become powerful prayer warriors and intercessors. Walking in spiritual maturity.

Advance in the word of God by encouraging the people of God to be ever diligent in their study of the Bible.

Nurture a burden for lost souls to be birthed into the Kingdom of God through the ministry of travail and intercession.

Develop true worshipers by teaching how to daily rise above the veil of the flesh, and enter through the auspices of the spirit, into the very throne room of God (the "most holy place").

Demonstrate the unconditional love of God in reaching out to those in need of help, hope and redemption.

Strengthen godly homes and marriages by promoting harmony and wholeness in the family.

Teach the people of God to walk in holiness and humility before God and man, possessing their vessels in sanctification and honor.

Challenge the people of God to fulfill their life's maximum potential as sons and daughters of God.

Help the people of God to receive and to operate in the zenith of the anointing and power of the Holy Ghost.

Minister health, wholeness and the peace of God to the emotional, spiritual, and physical well-being of hurting mankind.

Empower the people of God in leadership to rise to new heights of success through prayer and intercession.

Advocate unity in the Body of Christ by embracing them together in an interdenominational fellowship of prayer.

Support the ministry of Pastors and the work of the local church.

Establish affiliated units of praying people, beginning in the Dallas Metropolitan area of Texas and spreading throughout the nation and the world.

To experience the anointing and teachings of Apostle Donald and Prophetess Frances Cleveland, please join them for intercessory prayer with Hannah's Sons and Daughters at: Hannah's Sons and Daughters International Prayer Ministry.

Monday night, 7pm—9pm

Every Saturday, 5am—7am

Mailing Address:

Breaking of Day Family Church International

Hannah's Sons and Daughters International Prayer Ministry

P. O. Box 2811

DeSoto, TX 75123-2811

bodfc@yahoo.com

http://www.hannahssonsanddaughters.com

These prayer sessions are designed to empower your life and stir up the spirit of prayer within you. This is a strategic warfare intercessory prayer ministry that functions out of a global mentality. Prophetic Intercession is birthed each week as the intercessors lay prostate before the Lord.

Anointings, callings, and giftings are stirred up within these gatherings. If you want to be changed, charged, and challenged, join Apostle Donald and Prophetess Cleveland along with Hannah's Sons and Daughters in prayer during one of their prayer sessions.

See you next week!

About the Author

Prophetess Cleveland is an anointed prophetess who advances the kingdom through speaking to the needs and gifts in the body of Christ. She has become a noted subject matter expert, she and her husband, Apostle Donald Cleveland, Sr., also joined other ministerial collaborators in joint authorship of a book named, "Empowering your City Releasing the Apostolic and Prophetic Destiny of a City". She has been in the ministry for over 31 years during which time she has traveled throughout the United States. Her unique presentation of the gospel has enabled her to minister to many denominations and organizations, and as a result, she is a much sought after prophetess, teacher, leader and counselor. Prophetess Cleveland has served in leadership positions of presidential and directorship capacity while working and supporting the ministries of the late Superintendent Edward Calloway and Bishop T. D. Jakes. She sponsors and hosts an annual Intercessory Prayer and Travail Conference for those who have a hunger for God's presence and purpose. She is the founder and chancellor of Hannah's Prophetic School of Prayer, where she conducts in a scholastic environment to teach, train, and mentor those called of God for such a time as this. Prophetess Cleveland serves as Co-Pastor alongside her husband, Apostle Donald Cleveland, Sr., founder of Breaking of Day Family Church. She also serves on the governing board of Jabez Ministries of Dallas, Texas. She has received numerous awards, most noteworthy among them, the Intercessor of the Year, awarded by Lancaster Interdenominational Ministerial Alliance, of Lancaster, Texas. Her curriculum vitae include: Apostolic/Prophetic Intercessor, Evangelist, Teacher, Conference and Seminar Host/Speaker, Counselor, Outreach minister, Revivalist and Author. Prophetess Frances Cleveland has been married to Apostle Donald Cleveland for 37 years. They are the proud parents of three and grandparents of four. She is also the owner and director of her own business, "Fran's Creative Crafts."